LEAP THIRTY

*Poems*

DIANE LOWELL WILDER

*Diane Lowell Wilder* (signature)

JUNE ROAD PRESS
BERWYN, PENNSYLVANIA

Copyright © 2021 Diane Lowell Wilder

All rights reserved. No part of this book may be reproduced or transmitted without prior permission from the publisher, except as quotations for the purposes of critical review.

Cover art: Wilder Francone
Author photo: Lane Wilder
Editing and design: Sara June Arnold

ISBN 978-1-7356783-3-7 (paperback)
ISBN 978-1-7356783-4-4 (ebook)
Library of Congress Control Number: 2021937490

Published by June Road Press, LLC
P.O. Box 260, Berwyn, Pennsylvania 19312
juneroadpress.com

First paperback edition 2021

10 9 8 7 6 5 4 3 2 1

CONTENTS

1.
- 1 Vertigo
- 3 Diorama
- 5 Landlocked, 1971
- 7 Lifeguards
- 9 Dancing Queen
- 11 Glorious Leap Thirty

2.
- 15 Ex-
- 17 Moves
- 19 Room 214
- 21 Embodied
- 23 Takeout
- 25 Salad Nights
- 27 Voyeur

3.
- 30 Provisions
- 33 My Parents Throw a Party
- 35 Old Golds and Black Walnuts
- 37 Partridge
- 39 Cactus
- 41 Memento Mori
- 43 Reproduction

4.
- 47 The Beet
- 49 Triptych
- 51 Omelette
- 53 Chalk and Release
- 55 Mother-Fear

5.
- 59 Mud Season
- 60 Renovation
- 62 Blink
- 65 The Way Out
- 67 Hopscotch

## INTRODUCTION

Some poems are windows, little illuminations, strangers' houses lit at night. If we enter the right one at the right time, what might we discover or come to know—about ourselves, about the experience of others, about how to make our way in the world? Some poems are departures or arrivals, a push or pull toward a place or idea or truth. Some are brief dances, spaces for movement and expression and exploration. I think of them all as invitations: come inside, look at this, join me, head that way, let's see where this might lead.

This book is intensely personal, but it isn't autobiographical. These are, and these are not, my parents. My mother never smoked. I've ignored the fact of my brother; my sister only flits through. My strong and gorgeous daughters, by birth and marriage, have been compressed into a singular presence. These poems are built from memories as raw materials, shaped and reconstructed in such a way that, I hope, they take on forms that might be entered and embodied by others, able to summon a reader's own sense of self and history and direction.

I hope you'll find some points of entry and connection among the poems in this collection. I hope you'll join me in these leaps across time and space as I try to follow the shifting shape of selfhood and explore the boundaries of memory in the strange and surprising way that poetry uniquely enables.

*1.*

## VERTIGO

Oh, I see how it will end—
this is the way of vision
cataracted, prismed—
as my father careens, a bent
gourd launched from his chair
toward the bathroom, each
afflicted foot taking him farther
from the stability his
windmill arms are seeking.
And this is my mother
in a red sweater—
in a perpetual dash
from kitchen to dining room,
intent on clearing away
the leftovers.

I'm served another slice.
I'm still hungry. I'm so full.
I'm moving
farther from this center,
I'm sitting quietly
as they gyrate,
I'm watching from
within this centrifuge
as they are
spun away.

DIORAMA

We planted these lilies
five years ago
outside the house
and they've survived.

I think of it like
a dollhouse inside,
filled with furniture
in one-twelfth scale,
with a table set for tea
and tiny parents
who move between
the rooms and years
while I play house.

The wallpaper changes;
the sofa grows shabby,
the toy dog disappears.
The flowers out front,
laid bare, are made of
toothpicks, tissue paper,
and clay.

## LANDLOCKED, 1971

When I roared my Schwinn down this town's
empty roads, invoking rural gods,
there was a joy in me like spark plugs.
Luxury was a nickel-apiece paperback
at the fall church fundraiser

and I would pick one of the seven
records that we owned
and put it delicately on the turntable,
thinking: when I have money
I'll have music that is mine.

When the house across the street
was lit at dusk, its curtains open
in that golden hour, I could
see inside your kitchen, where
the wallpaper was poppy red
and avocado and your dishware
looked unbreakable.

There might have been a time when
I slipped into that kitchen, licked
the plates and ran my fingers
down the wallpaper, feeling
embossed outlines come alive,
playing with the light switch.

LIFEGUARDS

August and water are thatta way
outta town: kids pedal full bore
in bare feet, pitched forward
on banana seats, arriving
already blued cold.

Peter and Everett hunch to fill
the chlorine filters, pouring
measured stink in holes
before the quarters slap
on Formica and the lockers
start to open-close.

They don't always get it right,
the off-board flips, the
backward jumps, the forward
somersaults calamitous,
the belly-flops, a chin
or forehead sliced.

Call it a day and the stragglers
push out from summer's
center in soaked towels
to their strung-out farms,
down dusty roads and sidewalks
that end too soon.

About that last back flip—
the stripes of your suit turn end
over end and halt when you hit
the board, that crack—your neck.
From this point on, undone,
you are gravity fed.
Peter hauls you to the side.
Everett helps.

## DANCING QUEEN

In my leotard, I whisper, Oh why
won't these boys dance?

Adrenalined on pent-up lust, I drag you—
lurch into my rhythm,

down and back, cantilevered to the linoleum
in your pearl-buttoned shirt.

Our polyester clings to every smell it can,
B.O. and smoke and nineteen

seventy-nine. Sweet tang of red spiked punch,
Love's Baby Soft and musk, and our feet

are sticky as we slow dance, caught up
in our bell-bottomed trance

as if we're here to stay. Don't shy away.
I'm still deciding what I want.

## GLORIOUS LEAP THIRTY

Glorious leap of thirty years, sleek-toed
jeté and arch of feet and then the meet
and slam of landing here beside the jar
in which I keep my youth: I was nimble,
I knew frolic, I once got that close to grace.

I had a dog named Honey, who would
lick my knees beneath the table, who
would live to twenty, who went blind
but still would stagger out to bark
and bark at the chickadees.

Launched flat-footed, forward-loaded:
now my knees refuse my weight
and as I fall the dog still tugs,
pulling, pulling at her leash.

2.

EX-

My therapist asks if I enjoy
       being a victim

I will make that mistake again
I will play for tips
I will play for your half
of half-uneaten sandwiches

Want and rage and rhyme

And not enough sympathetic ears
to sort it out

My goal was to extract myself

You know nothing of my desires

I always thought we didn't kiss enough—
we went straight to it
and we floundered

Now I know the source:
drought and thirsts
and drowning

There you go,

Needing a tall one
a large cold one
and one more for the road.

MOVES

This is the spot on the sidewalk
where the DJ set up.

Me, fifty-something, in a crowd of
twenty-somethings.

Nighttime with the bridge as skyline
and the traffic hushed on 95.

He looks entranced,
clutching his drink, coming close,

opening his mouth to tell me,
"You can really move."

On this city corner, sticky, I say,
"Let me show you how it's done."

ROOM 214

I delight in your voice
from my hotel room,
where I sit and exhale
as we stumble
and confess
and recover.

Our conversation veered
toward our interiors.
We held tight until we
loosened, plunging through
our years apart.

I try to explain what
it feels like to fall in love
with you again:

When did I first notice
that adolescent hummingbirds
cannot control their flight?
They arc and plummet

and recover as they
try to hover steady.
I used to sit and watch,
inhale as they tumbled
toward the hibiscus.

EMBODIED

I am waiting for him
while I watch other women
walk past,

some ripening—
as I was once—
easy in their flesh, taut,
taunting.

My body strains
to return to center
by limber memory

but my limp remains:
the longer leg goes numb,
the hip socket

sprouting occasional
seedlings of pain.

Today we will walk,
his hip higher
than mine,

and I will vine my arm
around the stake
of him,
tether my joints
and sway.

## TAKEOUT

My man—
unbox that idea,
the possessive,
the contrast of our skins,
the grafting—
has requested,
prone, at two p.m.,
that we find a restaurant
that is known for meat.

Time, as it does in dreams,
loops and whorls, imprints itself
on my eye, slides things loose,
syncs up the ice of the rink
and the meat of the man.

My daughter, grown,
tends to my grandchildren,
who clamor and scramble,
and then they too
are on the ice, fast-footed,
slipping. They hook me
with their shrieks.

And I know a man
is there in my back room,
basking, the white duvet
thrown diagonally, the line
of flesh and fabric liminal.

In dream time I leave
the ice, cross to the bed
and the man, my man,
to consider the menu
that he holds.

SALAD NIGHTS

You ask: What can I bring to this party?
Show up with three romaine hearts.

I cut your lettuce with a plastic knife
so the leaves will not turn brown.

My kitchen coughs up more ingredients.
Very: this, this, this

salad making—I dice on the cutting board
while you hold a carrot unsteady,

lopping slices scattershot until we're
joking, laughing, tossing ourselves.

Here is our love in the wrinkled leaves,
our currency the vegetable coins in our bowl.

## VOYEUR

Late at night she moves
in the glow of her kitchen,
where I see her bend
over the faucet and paint
the water on her arms and face
and use a paper towel to dry herself
and drop it to the floor.

She comes in and out of view
for hours, moving from the sink
to a doorway that I can't quite
see from my window.

Her hair is short and gray.
As she reaches overhead
to lift meals from the microwave,
I study the beauty of her limbs.

I see the dwindling stack of towels,
imagine the damp pile on the floor.
I wonder where her family is
and who might care for her by day.
Each evening, unseen, I am
with her on her route.

One night my husband says
that watching her
saddens him.

Imagine, he says, what it's like
to be unmoored from memory
and, more to the point, alone.

Alone? I say, and he's
still watching me.

*3.*

PROVISIONS

I. 2019

I slip my spare calories
into my mother's pocketbook,
imagine telling her:
buy yourself something nice.

Her fridge is ferociously full.
Cream cheese, bagels,
casseroles and stews,
her counters covered with
the good intentions
of family and friends.

My sister insists again:
Try the banana split
(a favorite once).
My mother freezes
over the chocolate syrup,
an impossible landscape
of ice cream beneath.
She begs off,
pushes her chair away,
the food untouched.

II. 1917

My grandmother, age ten,
thought dandelions delicious,
carried a kitchen knife
to pry each plant from hard
prairie soil. Brought them home
to sprinkle with vinegar.
Before the blossom is when
the leaves are sweetest.

III. 1975

Another dinner
when my mother
was especially upset.
Chun King Chow Mein from cans—
brittle noodles, wet celery
and water chestnuts—
scraped from our plates
into the trash.

Her pressed lips and hard eyes.
Pink dishwashing gloves and
one light on above the sink.
A yellowing bottle of Ivory soap.
She scrubs at the cans, ferociously
peeling their labels away.

IV. 2021

My mother said take it,
use it as a planter or
whatever. With a blade
I pare flakes of carbon
from the base and think
of all the cornmeal mush
my great-grandmother
cooked in this, served
with molasses and cream.
Remove the rust,
oil it inside. Test it out
on my electric stove.
Fill it, let the seasoned
iron turn the water
into air.

## MY PARENTS THROW A PARTY

My dream confuses matzoh balls with crackers
in the soup, hexagonal with divots on their sides,
in salty broth that's yellow, flecked with fat that
could be bits of clams, which are also in the stew.

People are pushed away by wrong inflections,
the ones that warp a bit, the needle bumping,
skipping, jumping to the lines ahead. I love that
music. I profess as I agitate the living room to love
that turntable, those radio textures in the sky.

My father earned medals and was given kisses,
manly ones from men to men, and he was sought
for declamations, with sherry raised in glasses
high. And my mother was exquisite, a cathedral in
a cave, salty with her earthly love, so saintly she
could only tug at her hem when they came.

There was madeira that night, left in the decanter,
shards of almond cookies hanging on our lips. So
they kiss me goodnight with those sticky lips and
let the men descend. Confusion in the hall as to
what is egress and what is merely laundered linen,
as the air smells fresh like folded sun.

Doors bang open, doors bang shut, and then it's
sounds of skittering like a dog caught on marbles.

The sense of the body as the enemy, as a dragging
maw, talking and disgorging crumbs in an accent
I can't decipher. I will not forget its laugh, its good-
night chuck under my chin.

## OLD GOLDS AND BLACK WALNUTS

My parents gave me a basket
that once held black walnuts.
I cannot remove the smell
but I can fill and then empty it
as often as I want.

Visiting, I learned
that I am being played.
I play along.
We love each other
nonetheless.

She saved the dress she wore
the night she met my father
outside smoking Old Golds,
when they got close enough
that ashes dropped
and burned two snail holes
in her skirt.

Looking through the holes,
I can see the steps outside the club
and smell the smoke.

PARTRIDGE

My father
carries the saw.
We bicker
and trudge.
My mother says no
to each tree.

One year I'm old enough to
pick my own ornament:
a fragile partridge
caked with sequins.

One year my little sister
can't unplug the lights
we've strung around the tree
and so she pries them
from the outlet with
a butter knife.

My father replaces the fuse
while my mother holds up the knife
with its blasted tip.
Oh, my partridge sparkles
when the lights
come back on.

CACTUS

It thrived in her house for
forty years of family: graduations,
weddings, turkeys, oyster stews,
the spouses and the rhubarb pies,
the grandchildren, two dogs.

Per instructions, I pinch
the succulent leaves, those
squeezable little mittens of gel,
to encourage growth.
The temptation is to pluck
all the buds, which is addictive.
I don't do it. I continue to nip,
encourage, water. Keep on
ascertaining soil health, maximizing
sunlight. Remember moderation:
it's susceptible to root rot,
blister, aphids.

Five years of this and nothing:
promises that never bloom.
With each new move,
the table, plant stand, desk,
it keeps on dropping buds,
its dangling arms still growing.
There is no evidence
that this will change.
I've moved it to
a dark corner.

On our last call, she
finally asked.
"Great," I said.
"It's doing great."

MEMENTO MORI

I.

She will live to one hundred and three.
She will teach me how to hunt mushrooms
       and quote Marcus Aurelius.
She has written a poem that I will discover
       long after her death
       in a box of genealogy books.
            The poem is about me.
She will someday say to me,
       "When you know, you know."

II.

His last memory will be of snow clinging to mittens
       as Lewy body dementia tirelessly
       removes the other seasons
            from his seventy-eight years.
He will lose three of the fingers on his right hand
       before the age of five.
            He will learn to use his left.
He will be arrested in the Las Vegas airport
       for carrying a loaded gun onto a plane
       and be angry because
            this embarrasses him
            in front of his grandson.

III.

He will collapse at fifty-three, succumbing
       to a congenital heart condition
       that will kill his youngest son
            in another eighteen years.
This is the first photo I have seen of him.
He is a handsome man,
       which I know has allowed him
            to get away with things.

REPRODUCTION

curled,
the photograph
rocks in your hand,
old when you find it

you dream them
as they might have been,
the little boy's hand
still perfect
in the picture

seized, arrested
by what you see—
      a woman
      a boy
      a man—
and the guilty pleasure
of detective work

these three are now
becoming known,
reunited
even as they're
lost again

4.

THE BEET

My daughter
puts a beet from the garden
in a glass baking dish
    (canola oil)
    (425 degrees).

She
    takes
        a shower.

In the living room
I watch a show—
    a reboot of an old one, now with
    a heroine to slay the villains—
as upstairs
    the water runs.

A sweet smell—
charcoal and Girl Scout camp,
kindling thoughts of s'mores and sit-upons,
    tents shielding us from rain.

My daughter,
hair wrapped in a towel,
    returns to the kitchen.

The beet, as briquette,
    nurses flames.

Once we put out the fire,
debride the carbon hull,
    the beet
        at its center
    is moist and meltingly
        tender.

TRIPTYCH

Tell me the truth about you and Dad:
she says this as if she already knows,
tugging the shopping cart
nearer to the cereals.

Do you ever cheat?
She looks up from homework papers,
pushes them across the table,
eraser crumbs adhering to her arms.

Her tenth birthday dinner:
people curled asleep on steam vents.
She holds my hand tighter
and turns toward Love Park.

OMELETTE

I siphon my memories
into portions as they leak
from cracks, rheumy and slow,
each to its compartment,
distributing the amber yolk.
Cut the carton, hide the cups.
When they're rediscovered,
maybe plant them somewhere new.

A bit of my nephew's umbilical cord
and a couple of his baby teeth,
wisps from his first haircut
and his onetime favorite marble.
My sister looks uneasy
as I go to pour the contents
on the floor. I'm getting
organized, I tell myself. I'm
drinking plenty of fluids.

My daughter later rises onto tiptoes
after breakfast in her blue metallic clogs
to put my gift up on the kitchen counter:
seedling marigolds for Mother's Day.
She's crayoned across the carton
drawings of the two of us,
and we are holding hands.

CHALK AND RELEASE

On our laps the children nestle
with soft chalked feet and
bright red streaks of water ice
laced across their wrists and cheeks.
They have worn the chalk to nubs,
inscribing these stone steps
with loops and lines and names
that will stay until it rains.

My daughter, age three,
once announced that
reading hurt her brain
and asked me to remove
all the books
from her bedroom.

This: Put them to bed.
Feed them, bathe them,
wonder where one
has misplaced retainers
or sneakers or teeth.
Tell them:
wipe your mouth
and please—
be more careful.
Tie their laces
into double knots
that come undone
too soon.

MOTHER-FEAR

Two small boots lost on a tennis court—
expensive ones, left in the rain.

I find them on a walk one morning.
Take a picture to document

and send it to my daughter.
She asks if I have found the girl yet.

The girl hides: in the crib, in the pen,
in the tubes of paint I squeeze and distend.

The oil paint makes me high in my studio,
where the north light is naked and soft.

There will be a break, there will be a walk,
there will be the dog. I will get closer

to the boots today. I will look inside.
A label, a size, a name.

5.

MUD SEASON

The winter is long and caked with gray,
a time of bread and rough fibers

I hear your echo in the ice

There are pebbles in my shoe

Place one gently between
tongue and cheek

Spring will bring
boundaries of melt
and uncovered wells

Sink into the river, tilt your head
and breathe through reeds

The leaves have upturned
silver bellies

Imagine your thoughts rising
to the surface, pale yellow,
then saffron, then gold

Signal to me when
it's time

RENOVATION

I.

We walk the perimeter,
discuss the paint, the scrape

and burn of getting
this house ready.

There's the barn, its outside
garnet, its smell of hundred-

thirty-year-old pine boards
full of dry knots.

We are watching the land
through its cracks.

These slopes
of drawling beauty

are inviting us to stay:
imagine us here.

II.

The painter departs
in the van with sampled reds,

having evaluated the job.
There's the barn

and our house up on the hill
where there were orchards once.

He said it could be done
in a matter of weeks

if the weather stays warm,
if the fall doesn't come too fast,

but there's the possibility
it won't be done till spring.

I hold his estimate in my fist
as I wave from the porch.

You close the screen door,
a shadow behind the mesh.

BLINK

Thirty years is a blink, a quick
stroll as shade rolls over
our heads and clouds build up
to block the heat of our days.

We walked past homes and cars
and carried groceries, hefted
children, hired tutors,
drafted indignations.

We lost some things. We
accumulated treasures. We forgot
what we lost. We picked lint
from our pockets, surprised to find
blue kernels of seaglass.

We sat on the beach and tried to keep
the umbrellas wedged in the sand.
Got slammed and undertowed,
panicking once, and the kids laughed
before they realized
this was serious.

We hardly spoke.
We stiff-lipped.
We drank.
We liked the smell of smoke.

Every August, a constellation
of friends descended
to carry us on waves
of IPAs and microbrews
and the neighbor's
basement wine.

We liked the smell
of snow before it fell
and the ozone hint
of storms in early spring.

We could not distinguish
certain sounds of birds
and gave up identifying
them on hikes. The trails
we used to take became
too slippery to risk.

At night there was a hush
and desire to touch,
but our fingers stopped
just before our faces.
A decanting, all of it
sideways, then sidelined.

We sat and watched ourselves,
often thinking others must
be wrong. Often wondering
why we couldn't get enough.
Why we were flattened or
fattened by the sound of
laughter.

Thirty years of fingertips
poised inches from
each other's, our faces wet
with fog, salt breezes
blown from farther
down the shore.

## THE WAY OUT

You are fine with danger.
I just hug your neck, thinking:
this time you've returned.

When the nurse has gone,
you tell me that there's
all the time in the world.
Every memory will live on
whether we are here or not.

When I ask again if
you'd like to hear the story,
you nod from the bed,
so I start.

That day: we roared
and burst, consumed our
provisions—sustenance
for the slog.

When I find you again,
in the deepest blue of ice,
your voice becomes
a cavern.

The last image is always of your
hand holding unpacked snow,
your glove gone too.

You call for my help
to find a way out.
I hand you a sweater that you
can unravel, some threads
taut, some loose.
I feel you tug.

HOPSCOTCH

What are we if not
entangled?
What are we
if not bound
to one another
muscle to muscle,
four-legged,
tied to
specifics
of the hours,
boxed in by
the joy of rushing
to the sidewalk
and joining
in the game?

## ACKNOWLEDGMENTS

There's a sense that a poet's work is solitary, but nothing is further from my experience. I've been fortunate to have found a vibrant community of writers, from Marc Zegans, who encouraged me at the outset, to the robust Suppose an Eyes poetry group based at Kelly Writers House at the University of Pennsylvania and the workshop AKA Jane Doe, whose members helped me grow and improve. Thank you to Pat Green and those who heard, read, and critiqued some of these poems in their earlier forms. Special thanks to Ginny Badler, Ross Bender, Carole Bernstein, Navneet Bhullar, Sharon Black, Tom d'Egidio, Erric Emerson, Lucia Herrmann, Valerie Loveland, Jonathon Todd, Alan Toltzis, and Janine Van Patten, whose insights, expertise, and love of poetry have guided and inspired me.

Feedback from early readers Greg Davidson, Maria Simson, and Alex Stevens was essential to the evolution of this book, which would not exist if it weren't for my creative partnerships with Kate Danser Kelsen and Sara Arnold, publisher and editor of June Road Press. I am grateful, too, for the artistic input of my talented daughter, Wilder Francone.

DIANE LOWELL WILDER, poet, mother, former competitive ice skater, lover of jazz piano and languages, grew up in Vermont. She attended Swarthmore College and has had a long career in alumni relations and institutional advancement for liberal arts colleges. She lives outside Philadelphia and is active in the city's creative writing community. This is her first published collection.

JUNE ROAD PRESS is an independent publisher based outside Philadelphia. Founded in 2020, the small press aims to produce books of lasting resonance and literary value—explorations of time and place, journeys of all kinds—that lead readers to new encounters, connections, and discoveries, particularly from first-time authors and emerging writers. Find out more at juneroadpress.com.